GARSTANG

a pictorial history

Of related interest:
Phil Smith, *Real Lancashire: A journey through the history of the old county*;
Dr David Hunt, *Preston: A history* (forthcoming, 2009);
Dr Alan Crosby, *Lancashire: A history* (forthcoming, 2011);
Janet Hollinshead, *Liverpool in the sixteenth century: a small Tudor town*;
Peter Aughton: *Liverpool: A people's history*;
Stephen Bull, *'A General Plague of Madness': The civil wars in Lancashire, 1640–60* (forthcoming, 2009);
Malcolm Greenhalgh, *The River Ribble: A local and natural history*;
Peter Shakeshaft; *St Anne's on the Sea: A history*;
Professor John K. Walton, *Blackpool*;
David Brazendale, *Lancashire's Historic Halls*;
J. Lumby, *The Lancashire Witch Craze: Jennet Preston and the Lancashire Witches, 1612*;
Thomas Potts, *The Wonderfull Discoverie of Witches in the Countie of Lancaster.*

Full up-to-date details and secure online ordering at
www.carnegiepublishing.com

Garstang: A pictorial history

First edition, 2009

Published by Palatine Books,
an imprint of Carnegie Publishing Ltd
Carnegie House,
Chatsworth Road,
Lancaster, LA1 4SL
www.carnegiepublishing.com

ISBN 978-1-874181-61-3

Designed and typeset by Carnegie Book Production
Printed and bound in the UK by Information Press, Oxford

JOHN ASKEW
GARSTANG
a pictorial history
BANKS'S
ROYAL OAK HOTEL
JOHN CRO
SEEDSMAN
GARST
P

TEL
TO PRESTON
10½ MILES

INTRODUCTION

Garstang is an ancient market town on the western bank of the River Wyre, between the Bowland fells to the east and the Fylde plain to the west. The earliest written record of Garstang is in the Domesday Book, in which the settlement is referred to as 'Cherestanc'. The survey for the Domesday Book, commissioned by William the Conqueror, took place in 1086 and recorded all the land held by the king and his chief tenants, along with the resources that went with the land. This resulted in the production of two volumes known as Little Domesday and Great Domesday, which cover different areas of England. 'Cherestanc' was recorded in Great Domesday.

The Manor of Garstang existed for many centuries. The Lancaster family, barons of Kendal and Wyresdale, held it in the early thirteenth century. There is a record in *The Cockersand Chartulary* of William de Lancaster granting four oxgangs of land in Garstang to Cockersand Abbey.[1] Descendents of the Lancaster family retained land in Garstang in the late thirteenth and fourteenth centuries.[2] In the mid-fourteenth century, plague spread across Europe. Around 2,000 people died in the parish of Garstang between 8 September 1349 and 11 January 1349/50.[3] During the fifteenth and early sixteenth centuries, the Abbot and Convent of Cockersand probably owned the greatest part of the Manor of Garstang.[4] The 1501 *Rentale de Cokersand* – the bursar's rent roll of Cockersand Abbey – shows the extensive amount of property they held in the parish of Garstang at that time.[5] When Cockersand Abbey was dissolved in 1539, the manor went to the Crown, and shortly afterwards it was given to the Savoy Hospital in London,[6] which closed in 1702. On the expiry of a lease in 1738, the Manor of Garstang reverted to the Crown. In 1742, it was leased to Edward Walpole, a younger son of the first Prime Minister of Great Britain Sir Robert Walpole. As the lease was only for a short term, Edward Walpole was discouraged from making improvements to the town. A representation to George II resulted in an Act of Parliament being passed in 1749, which enabled the king to grant the inheritance of the Manor of Garstang to the trustees for Edward Walpole and his heirs.[7] The Manor of Garstang remained in the possession of the descendents of Edward Walpole until it was sold in 1919.

Garstang's Thursday market has existed since at least the early 1300s. In the fourth year of the reign of Edward II (1310), a grant was made to the Abbot and Convent of the Blessed Mary of Cockersand for a market to be held

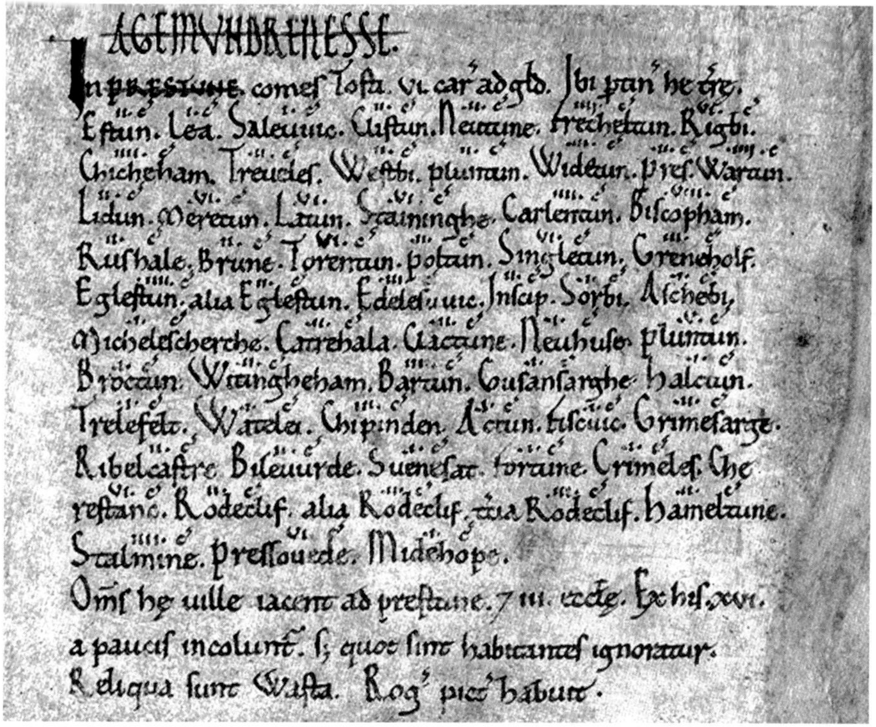
AGEMVNDRENESSE.
In PRESTUNE comes Tosti .vi. car' ad gld. Ibi p'tin' hec t're.
Estun. Lea. Saleuuic. Clistun. Neutune. Frechetun. Rigbi.
Chicheham. Treueles. Westbi. Plumtun. Widetun. Pres. Wartun.
Lidun. Meretun. Latun. Staininghe. Carlentun. Biscopham.
Rushale. Brune. Torentun. Poltun. Singletun. Greneholf.
Eglestun. alia Eglestun. Edelesuuic. Inscip. Sorbi. Aschebi.
Michelescherche. Catrehala. Clactune. Neuhuse. Plumtun.
Brocton. Witingheham. Bartun. Gusansarghe. Haltun.
Trelefelt. Watelai. Chipinden. Actun. Fiscuic. Grimesarge.
Ribelcastre. Bileuurde. Suenesat. Forton. Crimeles. Che
restanc. Rodeclif. alia Rodeclif. tcia Rodeclif. Hameltune.
Stalmine. Pressouede. Midehope.
Om's h' uille iacent ad prestune. 7 iii. eccle. Ex his xvi.
a paucis incolunt'. s; quot sint habitantes ignoratur.
Reliqua sunt Wasta. Rog' pict' habuit.

Garstang's entry in the Domesday Book: 'Cherestanc' can be seen at the end of the tenth and beginning of the eleventh lines. The Roman numeral above the entry indicates that the amount of land associated with the settlement was six carucates, a carucate being the area that could be ploughed by a team of eight oxen in a year. *(Reproduced with permission of The National Archives)*

on Thursdays in Garstang, and a two-day fair in June, on the vigil and feast of St Peter and St Paul (Peterstide).[8] The right to hold a market and fair reverted to the crown with the dissolution of the monasteries by Henry VIII. In 1597, Elizabeth I granted permission for a weekly market and two yearly fairs, one at Peterstide in June, and one at Martinmas in November.[9] On 5 August in the thirty-first year of the reign of Charles II (1679), a charter of incorporation was granted to the inhabitants of Garstang, making it a free borough and setting up a system of local government consisting of a bailiff and seven burgesses, known as the Corporation.[10] The Corporation elected a bailiff each year on Michaelmas Day, 29 September, at the Town Hall. The charter renewed the right to hold a weekly market on a Thursday and the two annual fairs. Following a meeting of the Corporation in October 1822, the fairs were proclaimed at the front of the Town Hall and at the Market Cross. In the early nineteenth century, cattle were also sold fortnightly between the first Thursday in Lent and Holy Thursday (Maundy Thursday).[11] In 1830, a new fair was introduced to be held in April for the sale of 'meat, cattle, horses, sheep, pigs, wares, and merchandise'.[12] The April fair in 1833 was a great success, with large quantities of cattle being sold. It was reported in *The Preston Chronicle* that, 'The expectations formed at its establishment, have been more than realized ... no doubt remains of its being one of the best Spring Fairs in the north of England.'[13] At Candlemas in the winter, a fair was held for the hiring of servants.[14]

The Peterstide fair was well attended in the early nineteenth century. Wool, sheep and lambs were the principal commodities traded at the fair.

The proclamation of the Peterstide fair of 1839 has survived:

> Thomas Walker Clarke Gentleman Bailiff of this Borough and Corporation of Garstang Doth in her Majesty's Name make open Proclamation that the Fair to be holden and kept in this Town is to Continue for two days ... And that all People so Resorting to this Fair do preserve and keep her Majesty's Peace upon Pain that every Knight shall forfeit Twenty Pounds, every Esquire Ten Pounds, every Gentleman Five Pounds, and every other Inferior Person Fifty Shillings ...[15]

By the 1870s, the Peterstide fair had lost its importance. In 1877, it was said that 'a lighted candle would be needed to find it', although a few lambs were sold.[16] The Peterstide fair of 1883 was proclaimed by the Corporation, but no dealers or buyers turned up, so the ancient fair finally came to an end.[17]

The Martinmas fair was an important annual event in Garstang. Dealers and buyers from all over Britain came to the fair, and in the evenings, the inns of the town were packed to the doors. Cattle were sold on the first day of the fair, while horses were sold and farm servants were hired on the second day.[18] In the early nineteenth century, between 2,000 and 3,000 cattle were brought to the fair at Garstang. There were entertainments for the people attending the fair, including hobbyhorses and shooting galleries, and there were stalls selling punch, cakes, gingerbread and nuts.[19] In the late nineteenth century, there were also photographic studios and 'travelling medicants'.[20] The last Martinmas fair was held in 1932. Just over 40 Irish cattle were sold on the first day, and only a single horse was offered for sale on the second day, which remained unsold.[21]

After serving the town for over 200 years, the Corporation of Garstang was dissolved in 1886 under the Municipal Corporations Act of 1883, the last recorded bailiff in the Corporation records being William Chapman in 1884. Garstang Town Trust was established in 1889 to administer the property of the dissolved Corporation, using the income from fair tolls and market tolls.[22] The property included the Town Hall and artefacts such as two constable's halberds and a silver-topped staff. The Local Government Act of 1894 established Garstang Rural District Council, which was abolished in 1974 when the district became part of the Borough of Wyre.

Garstang was situated on the main north-western route between London and Edinburgh, and the many inns in the town provided rest and refreshments for travellers and stabling for horses. In the late seventeenth and early eighteenth centuries, Celia Fiennes rode side-saddle through every English county, accompanied by only two servants. She was born in 1662, a daughter of Colonel Nathaniel Fiennes, a Parliamentarian officer. She recorded her journey through Lancashire and her visit to Garstang around 1698:

> … and here it was I was first presented wth ye Clap bread wch is much talked of made all of oates. I was surpris'd when the Cloth was Laid, they brought a great Basket such as one uses to undress Children with and set it on the table full of thin waffers as big as Pancakes and drye that they Easily breake into shivers, but Coming to dinner found it to be ye only thing I must Eate for bread. Y^{e} taste of oate bread is pleasant enough and where its well made is very acceptable, but for ye most part its scarce baked and full of drye flour on ye outside.[23]

In November 1715, the Jacobite Army passed through Garstang *en route* for Preston. The event was recorded by a contemporary historian, the Rev. Robert Patten: 'The Day proving rainy, and the Ways deep, they left the Foot at a small Market-Town called Garstang, half-way between Lancaster and Preston: Here the unfortunate Mr. Muncaster join'd us, who was afterwards executed, yet died very Penitent, and own'd King George for his only lawful Sovereign …'[24] Roger Muncaster was an attorney at law and town clerk, and was executed at Preston on 27 January 1715/16.[25] Three other local people who joined the rebellion were later executed at Garstang. Their burial on 16 February 1715/16 is recorded in the Parish Registers of Garstang St Helen: 'Mr Joseph Wadsworth and Thomas Goose of Catterall, Tho Cartmell of Claughton, Rebels'. The Jacobite Army again passed through Garstang in November 1745. In December they retreated northwards and were pursued by the king's forces:

> By advices from Preston, of the 14th, Major-General Oglethorpe, with his cavalry, was at Garstang that morning, and was to advance that night with his whole corps, and post his regulars on Elhil Moor, which begins about three miles on this side Lancaster, and extends beyond the town, and his irregulars were to be detached in small patroles, supported by parties of the regulars, with orders to attack any patroles of the rebels which they might fall in with. If the rebels marched off, General Oglethorpe was to pursue them and fall upon their rear, giving notice immediately to Major Wheatly, who was posted at Garstang with a considerable body of dragoons, to support him, and the Major was to be supported by the troops from Preston.[26]

From the eighteenth century, newspapers provide an important record of events in Garstang. For example, there is an early account of an incident in Garstang in *The London Chronicle or, Universal Evening Post* of 6–8 January 1761:

> *Extract of a Letter from Garstang in Lancashire, Jan. 4, 1761.*
> This morning, about four o'clock, I was waked with the dreadful cry of fire. As soon as I arose, I saw (oh! dreadful sight!) the late Mr. Styth's pretty house, so much in flames, that no person durst attempt any assistance. The house, with his library of books and papers (among which was the charter of the town) were entirely consumed. A few hours before the

One of the earliest known photographs of Garstang is this view of the High Street taken before 1865. The fish stones can be seen in front of the Market Cross, close to where the well and pump used to be.[27] This photograph was produced as a postcard in the early twentieth century.

> fire was discovered, we had a most violent storm of wind; but just at the unhappy hour the wind was as calm as if it had received orders to stand still; otherwise this poor little town must, in all probability, have been reduced to ashes, the houses (you know) being mostly thatch'd, no engines in the place, and water (excepting what was drawn from deep wells) at a great distance. We look upon ourselves as saved by providence: May we deserve such mercies.

Often the first indication of what the buildings and people of Garstang looked like comes from old postcards. They illustrate many aspects of social history, including the clothes people wore, the transport they used, and the houses and shops in which they lived and worked. Picture postcards were first published in Great Britain in 1894. Until 1902, the message was written on the same side of the postcard as the picture, with the address and the stamp on the other side. In 1902, the Post Office allowed the message to be written on the same side of the postcard as the address, so that the picture could take up the whole of the other side. Due to the popularity of postcards in the Edwardian era, many different views were produced, which has left an extensive photographic record of life at that time. Three people who produced real photographic postcards of the Garstang area were Herbert Jackson, Frank Crosland and John Towers.

Frank Crosland's photographic studio on the Promenade, Arnside.

Jonathan Herbert Jackson, known as Herbert Jackson from his postcards, was born in Garstang in 1863. Around 1835, his grandfather, Jonathan Jackson, built a cotton mill on the River Calder with his brother Richard, establishing the village of Calder Vale.[28] He lived at Vale House with his family. His sons, including Herbert Jackson's father, James Jackson, succeeded their father in running the mill at Calder Vale.[29] By 1861, James Jackson and his family were living at Dimples, a large and ancient house on Dimples Lane in Barnacre-with-Bonds, with his wife Martha's parents, Jonathan Labrey, a tea dealer, and Martha Labrey. In 1871, James Jackson is recorded on the census as a cotton manufacturer, employing 225 hands, and a farmer of 242 acres, employing 9 men and 1 boy. Herbert Jackson was brought up at Dimples. In 1881, aged 17, Herbert Jackson was a grocer's apprentice living in York. By 1891, he was a photographic artist living in Cleckheaton and he married Clara Eleanor Wilkinson from York in 1892. Although he lived and worked as a photographer in Yorkshire, Herbert Jackson also photographed many villages in the Garstang area. He produced hundreds of different postcards in the Edwardian era, some using earlier photographs from the late nineteenth century. Herbert Jackson produced some of the most beautifully composed and clear postcards of the Garstang area. They can be recognised from his small, neat captions, and from his address, which is present on the back of some of his postcards: 'H. Jackson, Station Approach, Cleckheaton. Further copies can be had at any time.'

John Towers, the photographer.
(Reproduced with kind permission of his grandson, John Towers)

Frank Crosland was born in 1856 in Stoke Newington, London. His father, Edward Crosland, was originally from Bolton in Lancashire, and his mother, Martha Blakey, was from Thornton Rust in Yorkshire. They married in 1845 at the Friends' Meeting House in Aysgarth, Wensleydale. By 1861, the family had moved to Little Horton, Bradford. At that time, Edward Crosland was an accountant and estate agent. By 1871, Frank Crosland was boarding at Sibford School in Sibford Ferris, Oxfordshire, the school having been established in 1842 for the children of Quaker families. By 1881, he had become a chemist's assistant in Liverpool. He married Mary Crossfield from Arnside in 1883. They lived at Mount Pleasant in Arnside, and Frank Crosland set up a photographic studio on the Promenade. He produced many postcards of the Arnside and Silverdale area as well as other places in Westmorland and Lancashire, including the Garstang area. His postcards often have distinctive, slanting captions, and many have his name stamped on the back.

John Towers was born in Nateby in 1863. His grandfather, who was also called John Towers, was a draining tile manufacturer in Cabus, and his son William began his working life as a tile kiln labourer. In later years, William had different occupations including fireman, sawyer and hairdresser. William lived in Garstang with his wife Ellen and their family, including their son John. When John Towers was older, he worked as a hairdresser and cooper from premises on the western side of the Market Place in Garstang. His son and grandson later continued the hairdressing business from the same premises. In 1887, John Towers married Mary Wearden, a fancy-goods dealer and dressmaker. John Towers produced postcards of the Garstang area from the early 1900s. The style of writing used for the captions on his postcards varies. A small monogram 'J. T.' can be seen on some of his early postcards, while others are unmarked. Around 1911, he produced a series of sepia-coloured postcards that are marked on the back 'J. Towers, Market Place, Garstang', some using earlier photographs.

As Garstang continues to change over the years, the postcards produced by these early photographers provide an increasingly important record of a bygone era. Each photograph represents a unique moment in time, capturing, for instance, a sunny market day, the tranquil Royal Oak Field, a long-gone tree or thatched cottage, all of which give an insight into Garstang's past. The postcards in this book have been arranged to give the reader a tour of old Garstang. Starting at Garstang and Catterall Station, the tour passes through Catterall, Bowgreave and Bonds before reaching Garstang. After viewing the streets and buildings of the town, the tour continues along the River Wyre, and then finishes in Barnacre and Nether Wyresdale.

Ordnance Survey map of Garstang, 1910.

GARSTANG
Acres 489·036
GARSTANG
Garstang Station
Engine Shed
Broom Hill
Hazelhead Wood
Higher Lingart Farm
Cross House
Slack Farm
Manor House Cottages
Manor House Farm
Wyre Lane
Lingart Lane
Watery Lane
Ford
Forge Wood
Forge Bridge
Forge Lane
The Forge
Lower Lingart Farm
Green Lane
Croston Barn
Back Lane
Lancaster 10
Garstang
LONDON & NORTH WESTERN RAILWAY
KNOTT END RAILWAY
Wyre Bridge
Parkhead Brook
Castle Wood
Beesley's Farm
Parkhead Bridge
Taylor's Bridge
Beech Mount
Smithy
Congl. Chap.
Sun. Sch.
Grammar Sch.
Crown Hotel
Market Ho.
Town Hall
Wheat Sheaf Inn
Church
Vic.
Liberal Club
Bonds Fold
Garstang Bridge
School
BONDS
St. Mary & St. Michael's R.C. Church
Church Inn
Garstang Mill
Mill Race
Aqueduct
Old Limekilns
Old Limekiln
Wharf
BASIN
Nateby Works
Ashfield
Moss Lane
Moss Lane Bridge
Gas Works
Stonefield Terrace
Cricket Ground
Saw Mill
Stout House
Garstang Road Bridge
Kettle Lane
Blackpool 16
Garstang
Many Pads
River Wyre
Greenhalgh Castle Farm
Greenhalgh Castle (In Ruins)
Greenhalgh Castle Lane
Old Clay Pit
Spring
Braid's Cottage
Turner's Bridge
Greenhalgh Castle Bridge
Dimples Bridge
Dimples Lane
Tarn Cottage
Greenhalgh Castle Farm
Turner's Bridge
Bailton's Bridge
Oaklands
Bond Villa
Garstang Turnpike Bridge
Byerworth Bridge
Byerworth Lane
Union Workhouse
Police Station
Garstang
Preston 10
Elmhurst
Byerworth Farm
Bowgrave Farm
BOWGRAVE
Beech Cottage
Friends Meeting Ho.
Calder Cottages
The Carrs
The Dimples
Blackfield House
Dobson's Bridge
Old Clay Pit
Bruna Hill
Calder Mount
Bruna Croft
Cross (Remains of)
Brooklands
Lodge
Garstang & Catterall Station
Ray Lane
Spring Cottages
Ray Lane Bridge
Little Calder River
Howarth
Sheepwash
Cross House
Pump House Farm
Hagg Wood
N D

CATTERALL, BOWGREAVE

AND BONDS

Garstang and Catterall Station and the Kenlis Arms Hotel *(photographed by J. Towers, around 1905)*

Garstang and Catterall Station opened in 1840 and for 30 years was the only railway station to serve Garstang. During that period it was known as Garstang Station. It was renamed Garstang and Catterall Station in 1870, following the building of the Garstang and Knott End Railway, and the opening of Garstang Town Station just to the north of the town. The Earl of Bective, who was previously Lord Kenlis, built the Kenlis Arms Hotel in 1871 on land belonging to the Barnacre Estate.[30] His maternal grandfather, Alderman Thompson of Underley Hall near Kirkby Lonsdale, had bought the estate from the eleventh Duke of Hamilton in 1853.[31] The Earl of Bective lived at Underley Hall and was known to drive around in a carriage pulled by four horses, with postilions in white buckskin breeches. He and his friends used the Kenlis Arms Hotel during the shooting season. Being close to Garstang and Catterall Station, the Kenlis Arms was a convenient hotel for commercial travellers, as well as tourists and picnic parties. There were regular sales of cattle and sheep at the hotel.[32] At the time this photograph was taken, the hotel's proprietor was William Titterington.

Kenlis Arms Hotel *(posted 1910)*

Lord Kenlis paid his first visit to his Barnacre Estate on Wednesday, 13 December 1865.[33] He arrived at Garstang Station and was met by his agent for the Barnacre property, his tenants and some other local people. An archway, covered with evergreens, streamers and the inscription 'Welcome', had been put up near the station to greet Lord Kenlis. He rode a horse from the station to a nearby house named Woodlands, where a second, larger archway spanned the road. This archway must have looked spectacular as it was decorated with evergreens, two large flags and the inscription 'Welcome' beneath a baron's coronet and the monogram 'K'. From a temporary platform, one of his tenants read an address, written on vellum and illuminated with gold, which was afterwards presented to Lord Kenlis. He then went on an inspection of his cottages and farms, which were decorated with flags. A flag had also been put up on a pole on the ruins of Greenhalgh Castle, which Lord Kenlis also owned.

'Jubilee Queen' engine, Garstang and Knott End Railway *(photographed by J. Towers, around 1907)*

The Garstang and Knott End Railway, initially linking Garstang and Catterall Station to Pilling, was opened in 1870. On Wednesday, 14 December 1870, to celebrate the opening of the new railway, the directors and shareholders of the Garstang and Knott End Railway, accompanied by the Scorton brass band, travelled to Stakepool for luncheon at the Gardeners Arms Inn[34] (now known as the Elletson Arms Hotel). In the afternoon, they returned by train to Garstang and the Inauguration Dinner was held at the Royal Oak Hotel. The 'Jubilee Queen' was the fifth engine to work on the Garstang and Knott End Railway, and was purchased from Hudswell, Clarke and Company of Leeds in 1897,[35] the year of Queen Victoria's Diamond Jubilee. In 1900, a similar engine called 'New Century' was purchased for the railway. The engines and carriages were painted a dark-brown colour. The extension of the railway to Knott End was completed in 1908. In the summer, the employees of the railway used to make hay by the side of the track. The cut grass was loaded into a goods wagon, which was pushed by hand along the railway to a nearby station, where it was offloaded onto a haystack. The railway closed to passenger traffic in 1930, following increased competition from road transport.

Arrival of Territorial Forces at Garstang and Catterall Station *(June 1911)*

In June 1911, between 14,000 and 15,000 East Lancashire Territorial Forces arrived for a training camp at Claughton near Garstang,[36] under the overall command of General Park, the East Lancashire Divisional Commander. Advanced parties of soldiers were responsible for pitching living tents, store tents and a dining tent, in preparation for the arrival of the main body of soldiers. The troops undertook various military exercises and instructional training. Small groups of soldiers were taught scouting skills, including map reading, elementary astronomy, sketching and signalling.[37] Manoeuvres took place over a wide area and included a detachment of cyclists skirmishing over the country between Garstang and Poulton. Towards the end of the two weeks' training, the military exercises had to be curtailed due to bad weather. Many troops bivouacked on the hills where fires were lit to dry their clothes, while others slept on waterproof sheets under walls and banks by the roadside, before receiving the order to return to camp.[38] General Park released a critical statement after the camp had finished, pointing out that some of the troops had given their positions away during the military exercises as they were silhouetted against the skyline.[39] He also reminded some of the officers, who had used motorcars and had servants present during the manoeuvres, that such luxuries would not be possible in a real state of war!

Brockholes Arms, Claughton *(photographed by G. Cross, around 1906)*

Catterall Post Office *(around 1904)*

Catterall Cottage *(photographed by J. Towers, posted 1914)*

Catterall Cottage was built in the latter half of the eighteenth century.[40] By 1850, Martha Boys, widow of George Boys of Broughton, was living there with her family and servants. Martha died in October 1863. Her son, William Boys, exhibited a wide variety of plants at local flower shows from the greenhouse and gardens of Catterall Cottage. In September 1873, at a flower show in Garstang, his exhibits included pelargoniums, fuchsias, exotic ferns, mosses, red celery and white grapes.[41] He died in March 1881, and the property passed to his sister, Margaret Boys. She died in January 1895, and left Catterall Cottage to her nephew, George Boys Stones. After studying at St John's College, Oxford, George Boys Stones became Curate of St Thomas's Church, Garstang, in 1878 and its first vicar in 1881. In 1914 he retired to Catterall Cottage. His daughter Alice wrote on this postcard, which was posted on 17 March 1914, 'This is the house where father and mother are going to'. George Boys Stones was Rural Dean of Garstang between 1916 and his death in 1923. Catterall Cottage had earlier been known as 'The Pickerings', and in the late 1970s became a hotel of the same name.

Bowgreave *(photographed by H. Jackson, around 1904)*

Bowgreave lies on elevated ground between Catterall to the south and Bonds to the north. Garstang Police Station can be seen on the photograph behind the tree at the top of the hill. It was built in 1855–56 at a cost of £1,300.[42] Some people were unhappy with the police station being sited so far from the centre of Garstang. One resident wrote to the editor of *The Preston Chronicle* in March 1857: 'Not a very long time ago the town was roused from one end to the other by a tramp knocking, with a large stone or stick, at almost every door. A similar occurrence took place again last night. A very suspicious looking man knocked almost everybody up, pretending to want lodgings, at about two o'clock in the morning. How is it that we are to be treated in this manner, and the police three-quarters of a mile away?'[43] There were annual inspections of the police at Bowgreave. On Tuesday, 28 February 1905, Lieutenant Colonel Eden accompanied by Colonel Moorsom, the Chief Constable of Lancashire Police, carried out the inspection.[44] Superintendent Hodgson, Inspector Harlow, 5 sergeants and 16 constables were on parade. The inspector was 'highly satisfied'.

The Carrs, Dimples Lane, Barnacre-with-Bonds *(photographed by H. Jackson, around 1904)*

Oaklands, Dimples Lane, Barnacre-with-Bonds *(posted 1912)*

Canal Bridge, Barnacre-with-Bonds *(around 1906)*

Travelling north from Bowgreave towards Garstang, the road crosses the Lancaster Canal via this bridge. A Scottish civil engineer named John Rennie was responsible for designing the canal. In April 1793, the Canal Office in Lancaster advertised in *The St. James's Chronicle or, British Evening-Post* for contractors to undertake the building of the section of canal between Galgate and the south of Garstang, including the building of an aqueduct over the River Wyre.[45] They also advertised for masons and quarry-men. The section of canal between Preston and Tewitfield opened in 1797. On the morning of Tuesday, 13 May 1856, there was a rumour of a screw steamer arriving at the canal wharf in Garstang, which caused as much excitement 'as if one of the new gunboats was being brought to the place, or as if a Russian fleet were coming'.[46] Hundreds of people lined the banks of the canal, and around noon the steamer arrived. It belonged to the Earl of Crawford and Balcarres, and brought about 100 people, who were his workers and their wives, on a pleasure ride from Preston. They had dinner and a dance at the Eagle and Child Hotel, before returning on the steamer to Preston. Around Christmas time in 1892, a thick layer of ice covered the canal and many people enjoyed skating on it.[47]

Bonds *(photographed by H. Jackson, around 1930)*

All the traffic travelling the north-western route between London and Edinburgh used to pass through the centre of Garstang. Until the mid-eighteenth century, road repairs had to be funded by the parish through which they passed. In 1751, Turnpike Trusts were created by Act of Parliament to raise money for ongoing repairs to the road through Garstang.[48] The money was raised by means of tolls, which were collected at gates that were put up across the road. In the nineteenth century, more people began to travel by train rather than by stagecoach. This lead to a dramatic loss in revenue for the Turnpike Trusts, and they were abolished in 1875 for the road between Preston and Garstang, and in 1882 for the road between Garstang and Heiring Syke near Burton-in-Kendal, the roads returning to local administration.[49] The amount of traffic passing through Garstang increased from 307 to 3,400 mechanically-drawn vehicles per day between 1911 and 1928, leading to increasing congestion in the narrow streets of the town.[50] A by-pass road was constructed to the west of Garstang, three contractors each building a different section. Two new bridges were built, and a third was reconstructed. The Garstang by-pass opened in October 1928. This photograph was taken from the canal bridge looking north towards Garstang. The road sign indicates that the photograph was taken after the opening of the Garstang by-pass.

Bonds *(photographed by H. Jackson, around 1904)*

On a map of the road through Garstang dated 1684, two properties are shown on the eastern side of Bonds Lane, just north of Dimples Lane.[51] These are probably the whitewashed cottage and the stone cottage on the right of this photograph. The southernmost property is labelled on the map as 'Y^e^ first hs of Garston'. The map shows that the road further south through Bowgreave was at that time surrounded by 'shrubs', no houses being present. In November 1905, Sir Thomas Lipton and the Prime Minister, Arthur Balfour, were motoring from Edinburgh when their car broke down near Garstang.[52] Not knowing who they were, a lady invited them into her cottage out of the cold weather, and asked them to take a chair by the fire, while the chauffeur was mending the car. They got the children of the cottage to sing school songs, and the lady served them a cup of tea and bread and butter. When the chauffeur entered two hours later and said 'The car is ready, Sir Thomas', the lady then realised that she had been entertaining no ordinary motorists! They gave her their cards and half a sovereign, and each of her children a similar gold coin. Mr Balfour said that he would be proud to see her if she ever came to London, and she would see the House of Commons.

Bonds *(photographed by H. Jackson, around 1904)*

The first Catholic chapel in Garstang was a whitewashed building situated off Back Lane, now known as Park Hill Road, and the first baptisms were recorded in 1788. By the 1850s, the old chapel had become too small for the increasing Catholic population of the area. The local Catholics, led by Father Michael Hickey, found it impossible to buy a larger plot of land in Garstang itself, but were successful in buying a site in Bonds from William Bashall.[53] St Mary and St Michael's Church, shown in this photograph, was built on the site in Bonds between 1857 and 1858. It was opened on Wednesday, 18 August 1858, a hot and sultry day, with the bishops of Liverpool, Salford and Nottingham in attendance. A choir from Preston assisted with the music, which included Handel's Hallelujah Chorus. Following the opening of St Mary and St Michael's Church, the old chapel was used as a warehouse for several years, and was then converted into the Garstang Institute, which opened in October 1865.[54] The Institute was used for local functions, including penny readings and concerts. Today, the building can still be seen with the arched windows of the old chapel at one end and the old priest's house at the other. The Church Inn, which can be seen on the right of this photograph, was known as the Rose and Crown Inn before the building of St Mary and St Michael's Church.

Interior of St Mary and St Michael's Church, Bonds *(photographed by J. Towers, posted 1913)*

Bonds Lane *(photographed by F. Crosland, posted 1913)*

Catholic gathering, Whitsuntide Festival, Bonds *(posted 26 June 1906)*

The way in which Whitsuntide was celebrated in Garstang changed little during the late nineteenth and early twentieth centuries. On Whit Monday, church services were held for the Protestants and Catholics, and a procession was held through the decorated streets of the town. The day concluded with separate entertainments for the Protestants and Catholics. On Whit Monday, 4 June 1906, after the morning processions, the Catholic children adjourned to a field off Dimples Lane, behind the Church Inn, lent by Mr J. Ibbison.[55] Meanwhile, the children of the Church of England and Nonconformist places of worship went to the Royal Oak Field, adjacent to St Thomas's Church, where they were served dinner, followed by games and sports in the afternoon, and dancing in the evening.

Sion Hill, Bonds *(photographed by H. Jackson, around 1904)*

The large house on the right of this photograph is known as Sion Hill. The Gardner family lived there for many years. During the night of Friday, 7 March 1834, when a solicitor named John Gardner was living at Sion Hill, the house was broken into via the dining room front window.[56] The thieves were thought to have watched the house from the barn opposite. Mr Gardner was alerted early the following morning when somebody noticed the blind outside the front window, and saw that the window was open. He found that property had been taken from the dining room, sitting room and office, where money had been removed from an iron chest and from a drawer in a desk. The stolen property included a large quantity of gold coins, Bank of England notes and silver coins, amounting to nearly £400. Two silver candlesticks, seals, penknives, pairs of shoes, and a tortoiseshell purse with a silver clasp had also been taken. Fortunately, the thieves had missed a safe, which contained about £500. A reward of £50 was offered for the apprehension of the thieves. In August of the same year, two men were convicted of the robbery at Lancaster Assizes and were sentenced to seven years' transportation. In 1901, Henry Roberts and his family occupied Sion Hill. Henry Roberts was a physician and surgeon, originally from Shaftesbury in Dorset.

Wyre Bridge and Garstang Mill *(photographed by H. Jackson, around 1890)*

A mill on the River Wyre in Bonds can be seen on maps dating back to 1684. On Tuesday, 3 February 1846, a man narrowly escaped with his life at Garstang Mill when the corn warehouse fell in, due to the heavy weight of wheat that had been delivered the day before.[57] Garstang Mill narrowly escaped fire in April 1859, as some turf that was used for drying oats caught fire under a large warehouse adjoining the mill.[58] Luckily, a man unloading his cart of cinders spotted the fire and it was put out without the aid of the fire engine. Richard Boys, brother of William Boys of Catterall Cottage, was the corn merchant at Garstang Mill for some time before his death on 23 March 1865. On 8 April in the same year, an advertisement was published in *The Preston Chronicle*: 'To be let, for a term of seven years, with immediate possession, all that well-established Water Corn Mill, called Garstang Mill, situate at Bonds, near the market town of Garstang, with excellent Dwelling-house, Farm Buildings, and about nine acres of meadow and pasture Land …' A fish ladder was installed at the weir for Garstang Mill in the summer of 1866.[59] In April 1893, following a long period of dry weather, a large number of salmon were seen above the weir, and many people visited Wyre Bridge to see them.[60]

GARSTANG

HEAL QUAR TERS
GARST NG DETA CHMEN
5th BA THE K GS OWN

Wyre Bridge, Garstang *(photographed by J. Rogerson, posted 1906)*

This photograph was taken from the southern part of the Royal Oak Field. The present Wyre Bridge, linking Bonds to Garstang, was built in the mid-eighteenth century.[61] It replaced an earlier bridge that had been built in the late fifteenth century by Thomas Stanley, the first Earl of Derby, for communication with Greenhalgh Castle. This earlier structure was said to have been high and narrow, with a watchtower for signalling with the garrison at the castle. By 1897, the surface of the present Wyre Bridge, which was paved with large cobblestones, had become very uneven. Cyclists regularly dismounted and walked over the bridge. One old resident said it was 'enough to knock the feet off horses and wheels off traps'.[62]

Bridge Street, Garstang *(photographed by H. Jackson, around 1904)*

Joseph Hartley was an ironmonger and coal merchant, and ran his business from a property on the western side of the Market Place between about 1864 and 1902. He was also land agent for the Garstang Estate.[63] After living for many years on the Market Place, he moved with his wife Ellen to Castle View on Bridge Street, which is the house on the right of the photograph with two bay windows. Richard Lang's business can be seen next to Castle View, with two men standing at the door. The business was originally established in 1814. In 1896, Richard Lang advertised that he was a plumber, glazier, painter and paperhanger, and also repaired bicycles and sold bicycle accessories.[64] In the early twentieth century, he began repairing motorcars and motorcycles. A new garage was built that could store eight motorcars. Pratt's and Shell motor spirits and Dunlop tyres were sold from the garage. Richard Lang lived with his family at Ivy Cottage, next door to his business.

Bridge Street, Garstang *(photographed by F. Crosland, around 1913)*

Bridge Street, Garstang *(photographed by F. Crosland, around 1900)*

Whitsuntide Festival, Bridge Street, Garstang *(photographed by J. Towers, posted 28 June 1907)*

In 1901, a correspondent of *The Preston Guardian* wrote 'It is only occasionally – excepting a little on the usual market day – that the sleepy ancient town of Garstang shows signs of animation, and one of the brightest holidays is Whitsuntide, when the processions take place.'[65] In the procession shown in the photograph, some of the children are carrying fans, while others are carrying banners reading 'Honour The King' and 'Obey Your Parents'. The Market Cross is decorated with flowers and foliage. On the morning of Whit Monday, 20 May 1907, the Oddfellows and Catholic Bretheren held short parades in Garstang, each led by a band.[66] Following services for the Oddfellows at St Thomas's Church and the Catholic Bretheren at St Mary and St Michael's Church, a combined procession was held through the streets of Garstang with the children of the town. After the procession, the Oddfellows had dinner in their lodge room, while the Catholic Bretheren had dinner at the Royal Oak Hotel. As usual, the Protestant children were entertained on the Royal Oak Field, while the Catholic children were entertained on a field in Bonds.

Bridge Street, Garstang *(photographed by H. Jackson, around 1904)*

For many years, the shop on the left of the photograph, with placards propped up outside, was a newsagents, printers, and Garstang Post Office. In 1861, a postman named James Cross, who worked between Garstang and Great Eccleston, received a suit of clothes from the inhabitants on his line of delivery as a mark of respect for his punctuality and courtesy. He wore it for the first time on St Valentine's Day, on which occasion, according to *The Preston Chronicle*, he had to deliver 'lots of love missives for the lads and lasses of the district'.[67] From 1863, the Wrightson family ran Garstang Post Office,[68] and the delivery of letters from there to Nateby, Winmarleigh and Cabus was introduced in July 1867.[69] In 1901, the census shows that Herbert Wrightson was the sub-postmaster and printer, and was assisted by William Johnstone. There was a frequent postal service, with letters arriving and being dispatched several times each day. The second cottage from the right was Fred Gardner's Boot and Shoe Makers, a business that had previously been run by his father Robert. Most of the thatched cottages on the right of the photograph have been demolished.

Church Street, Garstang *(around 1900)*

St Thomas's Church and Vicarage, Garstang
(photographed by G. Howarth, posted 1908)

Church Street, Garstang *(around 1906)*

The cottage on the left of this photograph in the middle distance was the Brown Cow Inn, which had the date 1685 carved over the front door. Septimus Smith, who was the proprietor in the mid-nineteenth century, had a passion for woodcarving.[70] The inn was full of curiosities, including carved chairs and cupboards, and a wooden chain, with a watch box and snuff box attached, carved out of an old gunstock. There was also a collection of about 300 crooked sixpences, which had been hoarded for good luck, and some ancient china. On the evening of 20 June 1893, a lion cub, about 12 months old, escaped from Sanger's Circus that was visiting Garstang.[71] It went to the Brown Cow Inn, where the landlord managed to shut it out. It then went down Moss Lane, pursued by several keepers, to the Gas Works, where it was recaptured, but not before biting a keeper in the leg. The Horns was another inn on Church Street, closer to the Market Place. During the nineteenth century, some large horns, reputedly dug out of a bog in Ireland, were attached over the door. These horns attracted travellers from the stagecoaches to the inn for refreshments, making the landlord, Jem Stuart, a 'rare profit'.[72]

St Thomas's Church, Garstang *(photographed by H. Jackson, around 1904)*

For many centuries, Garstang's parish church was St Helen's Church, Churchtown. St Thomas's Church, Garstang, was built in 1770 as a chapel of ease for St Helen's Church, replacing an earlier chapel that was situated north of the Town Hall. Until an organ was installed in October 1841,[73] the music at the chapel was provided by flute, fiddle, 'clarionette' and bassoon players.[74] In 1847, the chapel was re-roofed, the tower was raised, galleries were put up, and a burial ground was enclosed.[75] James Prince Lee, Bishop of Manchester, consecrated the chapel in 1848 in the name of St Thomas the Apostle.[76] Extensive alterations took place at the church between 1874 and 1875. A new chancel and organ chamber were added, the floor was replaced, and yellow pine benches replaced the old pews, which were described as having 'rather the air of horse boxes'.[77] The formal re-opening of the church took place on Wednesday, 3 March 1875. The church was assigned its own parish in 1881, the first marriages being recorded in that year.[78] This photograph is taken from the part of the Royal Oak Field that now forms an extension to the burial ground, which was consecrated in 1962. The Vicarage is behind the trees on the left of the photograph.

The Vicarage, Garstang *(photographed by J. Towers, posted 1906)*

George Boys Stones, the first vicar of the Parish Church of St Thomas, Garstang, lived at the Vicarage with his family for 36 years between 1878 and 1914.[79] His daughter Edith wrote this postcard, which was posted on 18 April 1906. She has recorded an interesting incident: 'This morning there was wild excitement as Dr Harrison's roof got on fire, luckily the far side away from Mrs H. The fire engine was got out with great speed and not very much harm was done except one corner being burned … This is just a new P.C. I think it is rather good.' Dr James Harrison, a surgeon and apothecary, lived at Wyre Bank, a large house on Church Street, Garstang. Wyre Bank had previously been the residence of his father-in-law, Dr William Chapman. Dr Harrison's marriage to Eleanora Annie Chapman, second daughter of Dr Chapman, was held at St Thomas's Church, Garstang, on 23 October 1890, and the wedding breakfast was held at Wyre Bank. The house later became the Masonic Hall and was demolished in 2007.

St Thomas's Church from the Royal Oak Field, Garstang *(posted 1919)*

Interior of St Thomas's Church, Garstang *(photographed by F. Crosland, posted 1910)*

Church Street, Garstang *(photographed by J. Towers, around 1907)*

The row of thatched cottages on the right of this photograph consisted of three dwellings. One contained a kitchen, back kitchen and two bedrooms, while two had only one bedroom.[80] They had outdoor closets, and the end cottage had a small garden, which can be seen behind the wall. Behind the cottages was a garden belonging to another property on Church Street, and behind this was a second row of cottages known as Cabbage Row. The site of the cottages is now occupied by the car park for St Thomas's Church, although the old garden wall of the end cottage has been partly retained. In December 1877, a statement was made at the meeting of the Rural Sanitary Authority regarding the keeping of pigs in Chapel Street (Church Street).[81] It was said that in some instances a person could put one foot in the pigsty and the other foot in the kitchen! People were supposed to keep pigs much further away from their dwellings and the Nuisance Inspector was authorised to look into the matter.

St Thomas's School, Garstang *(photographed by H. Jackson, posted 1904)*

St Thomas's School was built on land given by the Lord of the Manor of Garstang, Frederick Walpole Keppel, and opened in 1845.[82] In December 1865, a Christmas tree was put up at the school, which was decorated with over 200 toys.[83] Each scholar was presented with a present from the tree, and eight children who had attended the school most regularly and whose conduct had been good were presented with a more valuable item, such as a workbox or writing desk. More land was acquired for a playground in 1884, and the school was extended in 1901.[84] The entrance to Dr Harrison's residence, Wyre Bank, can be seen on the photograph to the left of the school. In March 1905, Dr Harrison's groom-gardener, William Lancaster, was charged with stealing 40 bottles of port wine, 3 bottles of old sherry and 4 bottles of old brandy from his employer.[85] His house was searched and some of the missing bottles were found. He was tried at Garstang Petty Sessions where he admitted the charge. Dr Harrison asked the Bench to be lenient as he had left his wine cellar unlocked, and William Lancaster had a wife and children. He was sent to prison for one month, with hard labour.

Royal Oak Hotel, Garstang *(photographed by H. Jackson, around 1890)*

In September 1873, a correspondent of *The Preston Chronicle* wrote 'Wonders never cease in Garstang. We have had a flower show this week, last week an agricultural show, and *mirabile dictu* [wonderful to relate] we have actually had the Fylde Waterworks Company laying pipes to supply the town with water. What next? Let us hope it will be gas!'[86] At that time, Garstang was lit in the winter by several old oil lamps, which were stored in a loft of the Town Hall during the summer.[87] The Garstang Gas Company was set up six years later in 1879 in order to light the town with gas, and the Gas Works opened the following year.[88] The ratepayers of Garstang had to pay the company an annual fee to light each lamp in the town. In September 1891, the fee was set at 30s. per lamp per annum.[89] For several years until its restoration in 1897, a gas lamp was present on top of the Market Cross. The remains of the gas lamp can be seen in this photograph. Before the opening of the railway in 1840, the main means of transport for long journeys across country was by coach. The Royal Oak Hotel was one of Garstang's principal coaching inns. Coaches would stop so that the horses could be changed and passengers could have refreshments. At the time this photograph was taken, Nicholas Isles was the proprietor. In an advert dating from 1896, he advertised 'Wines and cigars of the finest quality. Horses, carriages and hearses for hire. Best accommodation for cyclists. Hot and cold baths. Picnic and other parties catered for on most reasonable terms. Orders and telegrams promptly attended to.'[90]

Market Place, Garstang *(photographed by H. Jackson, around 1890)*

Isaac Storey, whose grocers shop can be seen on the photograph, died in 1895. His widow Ellen, assisted by her sons Frederick and Christopher, continued the business. Her daughters, Mary and Eleanor, were confectioners. Storey's Grocers sold products such as Colman's mustard and starch, Cadbury's cocoa and chocolate, Fry's cocoa, Quaker oats and Sunlight soap. The Town Hall, which can be seen to the left of the photograph, was built in the mid-eighteenth century, replacing an earlier building.[91] The lower room in the Town Hall was used for a corn market, while the upper was used for public business.[92] In September 1831, to celebrate the coronation of William IV and Queen Adelaide, 100 poor women were treated to tea and a taste of liquor in the Town Hall, paid for by public subscription.[93] Loaves of bread, a portion of cheese and liquor were distributed in the Market Place to the poor men, and buns were given to the children. The clock was placed on the Town Hall in 1847,[94] and a new weather vane was installed in 1858, after the former one blew down.[95] Garstang Petty Sessions were held in the building for many years until 1893, when they were moved to the Garstang Institute.[96] In January 1939, a fire severely damaged the Town Hall, but it was later restored.

Singing around the Market Cross, Garstang *(photographed by J. Rogerson, posted 1905)*

The streets of Garstang were decorated with streamers and bunting for the annual Whitsuntide Festival, and on other special occasions. Festivities were held on Wednesday, 4 August 1897, to celebrate the coming of age and visit of the Lord of the Manor, Bertram William Arnold Keppel of Lexham Hall, Norfolk.[97] In the Market House, 150 tenants and 250 schoolchildren assembled before walking down in procession to Wyre Bridge. Mr Keppel drove up in a carriage, the horses were removed, and then some of the tenants pulled the carriage from the bridge to the Market Place. The procession went as far as the Grammar School, before returning to the Royal Oak Field. The children were given refreshments, including coffee and oranges, and played games. The tenants were given tea in the Institute, following which Mr Keppel was presented with a silver bowl and an address inscribed on vellum.

Market Day, Garstang *(photographed by H. Jackson, around 1904)*

The Market Cross was restored by public subscription in June 1897 to celebrate the Diamond Jubilee of Queen Victoria. A stone ball was placed on top of the column, and elaborate brackets were attached to support a pair of gas lamps. The fête to celebrate the Jubilee was held on Tuesday, 22 June 1897.[98] A procession took place led by out-riders in fancy costumes, halberdiers carrying the Royal Standard, and the town bellman. Following these were local dignitaries, a band from Preston, the Knutsford Morris Dancers and the children of the town. Jubilee gift medals were presented to 700 children. The National Anthem was sung around the Market Cross with Dr Harrison leading the singing. In the afternoon, there were sports and dancing on the Royal Oak Field, and the children were given oranges and sweets. A tea was given to widows and those aged over 50 at the Institute. Dancing went on until the early hours of the following morning. Storey's Ironmongers and Oil Dealers is situated to the right of the archway in the photograph. During the late nineteenth and early twentieth centuries, James Sandham Storey was running the business, and lived on the Market Place with his wife Isabella and family. His grandfather, John Taylor Storey, was a draper and tea dealer in Garstang in the mid-nineteenth century. James's father, John Storey, began his working life as a tailor, and then later established the family's ironmongers business. All the children in the photograph are wearing clogs.

Market Day, Garstang *(photographed by H. Jackson, around 1903)*

This postcard can be dated from the sign above the shop front of the ironmongers across the Market Place, which reads 'Singleton late Hartley', indicating that the photograph was taken shortly after the business changed hands. Henry Singleton was a tin-plate worker. He married Nancy Kelsall on 12 June 1884 at St Thomas's Church, Garstang. Around 1902, Henry Singleton took over Joseph Hartley's Ironmongers that had previously traded from the same premises on the Market Place. Garstang's fire engine used to be stored in an outbuilding at the back of the shop, before it was moved to the Market House.[99] This postcard was written and posted on Thursday, 31 August 1905. The message reads 'We are for the present at Garstang as it is show day. Quite an old fashioned place.' Garstang Agricultural Society had been formed in the early nineteenth century and held shows from 1813, although there were many years when no show took place. The 1905 show was held in glorious weather and there was a record number of entries.[100] The categories consisted of cattle, horses, sheep, pigs, dogs, pigeons, poultry, cheese and butter, farm produce and horticulture.

Market Day, Garstang *(photographed by J. Towers, around 1908)*

A new pair of gas lamps can be seen on the Market Cross on postcards dating from around 1908. This photograph shows a busy market day scene on a warm, sunny day. John Towers' shop can be seen just left of centre and nearby there is a stall selling watering cans. On the right of the photograph, next to Edward Cartmell's Tailors and Drapers, is a bank, which was built on the site of a house that was pulled down around 1901. It had formerly been occupied by a veterinary surgeon named George Breakell and his family, who had moved to Bonds by 1901. In the nineteenth century, on market days in Garstang, it was customary for small groups of people to go to the provision shops, where they would be served tea with wheaten and oatmeal cakes.[101] Many farmers around Garstang kept sheep, and wool was a commodity traded in the town. Some fleeces were sold directly from the farmhouses, while some were traded at the annual Peterstide fair in Garstang.[102] In May 1906, agents of wool dealers and manufacturers from Yorkshire attended Garstang Market to negotiate with the local farmers for the season's fleeces.[103]

Market Place, Garstang *(photographed by F Crosland, posted 1913)*

There are reports in eighteenth- and nineteenth-century newspapers of Garstang being affected by severe weather. On Friday, 5 April 1799, after a day of exceptionally heavy snow, the Manchester and Liverpool stage and mail coaches travelling to Carlisle got stuck near Garstang, with the passengers having to walk to an inn in the town.[104] Early in the morning of Monday, 7 January 1839, Mr and Mrs Dobson of the Royal Oak moved from their bedroom during a bad storm, as they feared one of the chimneystacks would collapse. They had a narrow escape, as an hour later the chimneystack did collapse, and a large quantity of bricks and rubble fell onto their bed.[105] For several days in April 1859, the worst storm for many years affected the Garstang area.[106] It was at its worst in the early hours of the morning of Thursday, 28 April. Trees were blown down, and the streets of Garstang were strewn with thatch and slates. Almost half the houses in the town were down to bare timbers. The finial and cross on the new Catholic Church in Bonds were blown off, and the windows of St Thomas's Church were blown in. The weather vane on the Town Hall, which had only been put up the previous year, also succumbed to the severe weather.

Market Day, Garstang *(posted 1927)*

By 1927, the Market Cross supported road signs. In this photograph, the van that can be seen in front of the Market Cross belonged to Thomas Swarbrick, a potato merchant from Cabus. The message on the postcard, which was posted on Tuesday, 28 June 1927, reads 'Sir N. S. arrived yesterday. Says weather conditions for eclipse as bad as can be. We have a large party to view what can be seen of it, which is rather fun anyhow. Hope to see the Prince of Wales today as he goes through Garstang. Wish you were here.' The Prince of Wales passed through Garstang as part of his tour of North Lancashire.[107] Crowds of people gathered in the High Street, which had been decorated for the occasion. Local children sang patriotic songs, and the Prince smiled and waved as he drove past. He stopped his car, and shook hands with a number of ex-servicemen. The total eclipse of the sun took place on Wednesday, 29 June 1927. A large crowd of people gathered to view the eclipse on the railway embankment near Garstang Town Station and 500 people gathered on Beacon Fell. Although there was cloud around, some people had good views of the eclipse from the hills around Garstang.

Market Day, Garstang *(around 1903)*

Garstang's busy market days and annual fairs provided opportunities for thieves. At the Martinmas fair in 1842, Richard Kenyon, a cattle dealer from Chipping, was robbed of his pocket book containing £180, while he was drunk.[108] In November 1861, Mrs Bleasdale, a farmer's wife who lived on Barnacre Moor, attended Garstang fair with her son-in-law, for the purpose of selling a cow.[109] Her son-in-law sold the cow for £9, and Mrs Bleasdale put the money, in sovereigns, into her purse. After a few minutes, she discovered that the purse had been stolen from her pocket, but no trace of the thief could be found. On Thursday, 15 February 1872, two ladies had their purses taken while attending Garstang butter market, which was the sixth robbery in three months.[110] In April 1874, two sisters were each sentenced to 14 days' imprisonment for stealing from stalls on Garstang Market.[111] They had stolen a handkerchief and some other articles from the stall of Thomas Heyes, a pawnbroker from Preston, and some items of drapery from the stall of Thomas Blackburn, a fent dealer also from Preston.

Market Place, Garstang *(photographed by H. Jackson, posted 1910)*

There are reports in nineteenth-century newspapers of the shops in Garstang putting on good displays at Christmas time. One of the best-decorated shops each year was the Post Office, where, in 1876, Mrs Wrightson displayed a Christmas tree decorated with ornaments and presents.[112] The Post Office can be seen on the left of this photograph, next to the bank. The butchers also put on fine displays each year. In December 1881, they decorated their shops with holly and mistletoe, and displayed in their windows first-prize beef and mutton, along with suckling pigs with an apple or orange in their mouths.[113] In the shops of the poultry dealers, turkeys, geese and ducks were hanging in profusion. The drapers also decorated their shops with holly berries and mistletoe. Provision was regularly made for the poor of Garstang at Christmas time. On a cold, frosty Christmas Day in 1877, the 25 inhabitants of the Workhouse were served an old-fashioned English dinner, consisting of roast beef and plum pudding with zest, and were later served mince pies.[114] On Boxing Day, around 200 people sat down to a public tea at the Garstang Institute, in aid of the Widow and Orphans' Fund. Various entertainments followed, including the Misses Chapman playing 'Sleigh Bells' on the pianoforte.

High Street, Garstang *(photographed by F. Crosland, around 1906)*

Garstang Market *(photographed by J. Towers, around 1907)*

Garstang Market *(photographed by J. Towers, around 1908)*

Garstang Market *(photographed by J. Towers, around 1910)*

Market Day, Garstang *(photographed by J. Towers, around 1907)*

Seventeenth- and early eighteenth-century maps of Garstang show two market crosses, one in the position of the present Market Cross, and one in the small square in front of the present-day Kings Arms. The records of the expenses of the Corporation of Garstang include one entry for 'removing old cross' in 1754,[115] although it is not known which cross this refers to. The last night in April was known as 'Mischief Night' in Garstang. Mischief-makers used to take anything that was loose to the Market Cross, where they would create an 'exhibition' for May Day morning. In 1877, the display at the Market Cross included tubs, buckets, wheelbarrows, spades and two ducks,[116] while in 1879, a donkey was tethered to the Market Cross 'whose gentle braying rose very melodiously on the morning breeze'![117] In the early nineteenth century, there were 13 pubic houses in Garstang, including one called the Blue Anchor.[118] In July 1834, all the household furniture and stock-in-trade of Thomas Savage, landlord of the Blue Anchor, was sold by auction in order to pay his creditors. The auction was advertised in *The Preston Chronicle*: 'And the Stock-in-trade includes a quantity of Ale, Porter, Brandy, Rum, Gin, Bottles, Glasses, Measures, Barrels, Casks, and all kinds of Brewing Utensils. Also will be Sold, 1 good Cow, 2 Calves, 1 Sow and 8 young Pigs, and 1 Sow In-Pig. Likewise the Garden Crops, consisting of Gooseberries, Peas, Beans, Potatoes, and Apples.'[119] The Blue Anchor continued as an inn until 1870.[120]

CHEMIST
THOMAS
MARKET
GARSTANG

A charabanc outside the Eagle and Child Hotel, Garstang *(around 1920)*

Edward Walpole, a younger son of the first Prime Minister of Great Britain Sir Robert Walpole, acquired the Manor of Garstang in 1742.[121] Through his daughter, it passed to the Keppel family of Norfolk. The Keppel family first attempted to sell the Garstang Estate in an auction sale held in London in 1867.[122] The catalogue for this unsuccessful sale has survived, although the associated map is missing. It describes a property occupied by a lady called Margaret Hayhurst. She had a bonnet shop with a dwelling house, pigsty, and garden. Her daughter Elizabeth, who was a milliner in Garstang, died two years earlier on 16 February 1865.[123] Margaret's husband William died suddenly the following day while sweeping snow from in front of his house.[124] Father and daughter were buried together. The majority of the Garstang Estate was sold at a second sale, which was held in Garstang in 1919.[125] The catalogue and map for this sale have both survived. They show that many properties on the High Street had gardens off Back Lane. One plot of land off Back Lane was divided into 13 small gardens. The Eagle and Child Hotel is described in the catalogue. It was occupied by Mr T. H. Richardson and had a large yard, stabling and outbuildings at the rear. It also had a bowling green, gardens and orchards on land to the west of Back Lane.

Market Day, Garstang *(photographed by F. Crosland, around 1905)*

The Market House, which can be seen to the left of the Town Hall, opened in November 1845.[126] Before St Thomas's Church was built in 1770, Garstang's chapel was situated near this site. It was built in 1666, replacing an earlier chapel. The records of the Corporation of Garstang give some idea of what the seventeenth-century chapel was like, as they record the repairs that were carried out on the building and the cost to the Corporation.[127] It was a whitewashed building with a slate roof, a clock and a bell. There are several records of repairs to the windows. In 1776, Sir Edward Walpole leased the site of the chapel for 60 years to Joseph Clarke, an attorney at law, who built a house there. Other interesting expenses of the Corporation of Garstang include 'cash spent at Gunpowder and Treason' in 1752, 'repairing stocks' in 1756 and 'fixing fish stones' in 1767–68. The fish stones, which were situated just to the south of the Market Cross, had to be removed around the 1860s after burning tar barrels were put on them one November 5, which caused them to crack.[128] It was the custom in Garstang on the night of November 5 for local young men, referred to as 'hobbledehoys' in one newspaper report, to parade around the streets of the town carrying blazing barrels of tar and effigies, which were made to look like political and religious figures, and local people.[129] The parade would end near the Market Cross, where the effigies were burned to loud cheers, and firearms were discharged. Many local people were unhappy with the disorderly behaviour. By the 1880s the police quelled the annual parade, although people still enjoyed letting off fireworks such as squibs and crackers.

High Street, Garstang *(photographed by H. Jackson, around 1906)*

Stoops Hall, on the left of this photograph, was rebuilt in 1882. The Wesleyans used to hold services in a room in the old Stoops Hall before their first chapel was built in 1814.[130] In November 1875, a labourer, while repairing a drain behind Stoops Hall, found a gold coin dated 1715,[131] which was the year the Jacobite army passed through Garstang. He took it to Mr Thomas, a chemist on the High Street, who gave him a sovereign for it. The Pack Horse Hotel can be seen on the right of the photograph, opposite Stoops Hall. In February 1872, Robert Swindlehurst, landlord of the Pack Horse Inn, was charged with being drunk and permitting drunkenness in his own house.[132] Two policemen visited the inn on 2 February 1872. They found men and women dancing in the dancing-room, since it was Candlemas time, several men drunk in the parlour and the landlord drunk in the kitchen. He was fined £2 with costs. The field adjoining the inn was regularly used for bowling matches, and there is a record of a quoits match being held on Monday, 18 June 1883.[133] The inn lost its license in 1906, following an appeal, on the grounds that it was structurally deficient and the rooms were small, dark and had low ceilings.[134] It was also pointed out that there were too many public houses in Garstang for the small population of the town. The inn became a temperance hotel.

High Street, Garstang *(posted 1914)*

In 1756, Sir Edward Walpole granted to the bailiff and burgesses of Garstang a lease for 200 years (from Lady Day 1765) of an area of land known as Croston's Waste, on which to build a school,[135] which can be seen facing in the centre of this photograph. John Morland of Winmarleigh endowed the school with £150. The schoolmaster was paid an annual sum of £6 15s. for which he had to educate four scholars free of charge, selected by the town's bailiff.[136] Garstang Grammar School was described by Anthony Hewitson in *Our Country Churches and Chapels*, which was first published in instalments in *The Preston Chronicle* between 1870 and 1872: 'the interior was dirty, slovenly; there were a few old dingy maps on the walls, a wicked-looking old comb hanging by a piece of string near the door, books here and there, book leaves strewn upon the floor, and a lot of other odds and ends in a careless condition'.[137] Standards at the school had improved by the annual inspection of December 1873, following the appointment of a new teacher, Mr W. W. Parkinson: 'In reading, writing, arithmetic, geography, history and grammar, the scholars displayed an excellent knowledge, whilst the freehand drawing of a number of pupils elicited the highest credit. In mental arithmetic the surprise that the results could be obtained in so short a time was very great.'[138] The final lessons at Garstang Grammar School took place on Friday, 28 September 1928.

High Street (Lancaster Road), Garstang *(early 1900s)*

The whitewashed property on the left of the photograph was a public house, previously named the Swan Inn. On 26 March 1879, the thatched roof of the inn was damaged by fire.[139] It was renamed the Crown Inn around 1891–92.[140] The whitewashed building was replaced by the present brick building about 1912. Ben Fisher and his son David operated a boot and shoemakers from the cottage on the right of the photograph. John Fisher was a clogger on the same premises. On the afternoon of Sunday, 13 November 1831, a fire broke out in a row of cottages at the northern end of Garstang.[141] A turf-house caught alight, which, according to *The Lancaster Gazette*, 'exhibited a scene most awfully grand'. Local people used tubs, milk cans and carts to convey water to the fire. The fire engine, which had only just been repaired, was brought out. Water was sprayed onto adjoining cottages, which were beginning to ignite, to stop the fire from spreading. Luckily, the strong northerly wind of a few days before had eased. Two cottages, the turf-house and some stables were destroyed, but no lives were lost.

Wesleyan Chapel, Garstang *(photographed by J. Towers, around 1910)*

Garstang's first Wesleyan Chapel was built in 1814. By the 1870s it had become too small as it only accommodated around 120 people.[142] In 1878, it was described as 'like nothing in the heavens above, nor in the earth beneath, nor yet in the waters under the earth'.[143] The old chapel was pulled down in the first week of March 1878. The Rev. John Leathley was instrumental in the project to build the new chapel, and many members of his congregation gave money towards its construction. On Monday, 22 April 1878, a ceremony was held to lay the memorial stones for the new chapel and Sunday school shown in the photograph. Under one of the memorial stones, the Rev. John Leathley placed a bottle containing some coins, a description of the old chapel, and copies of *The Lancaster Guardian* and *The Preston Guardian*. The memorial stones can still be seen today. After the ceremony, a tea was held at the Garstang Institute, which had been decorated with evergreens and banners. Many of the stones from the old chapel were strewn over the footpath for many months as the new chapel was built. Several people fell over the stones during the dark nights of the following winter, prompting a complaint in *The Preston Chronicle*.[144] The new chapel could accommodate around 180 people, and the Sunday school could accommodate around 140 children.

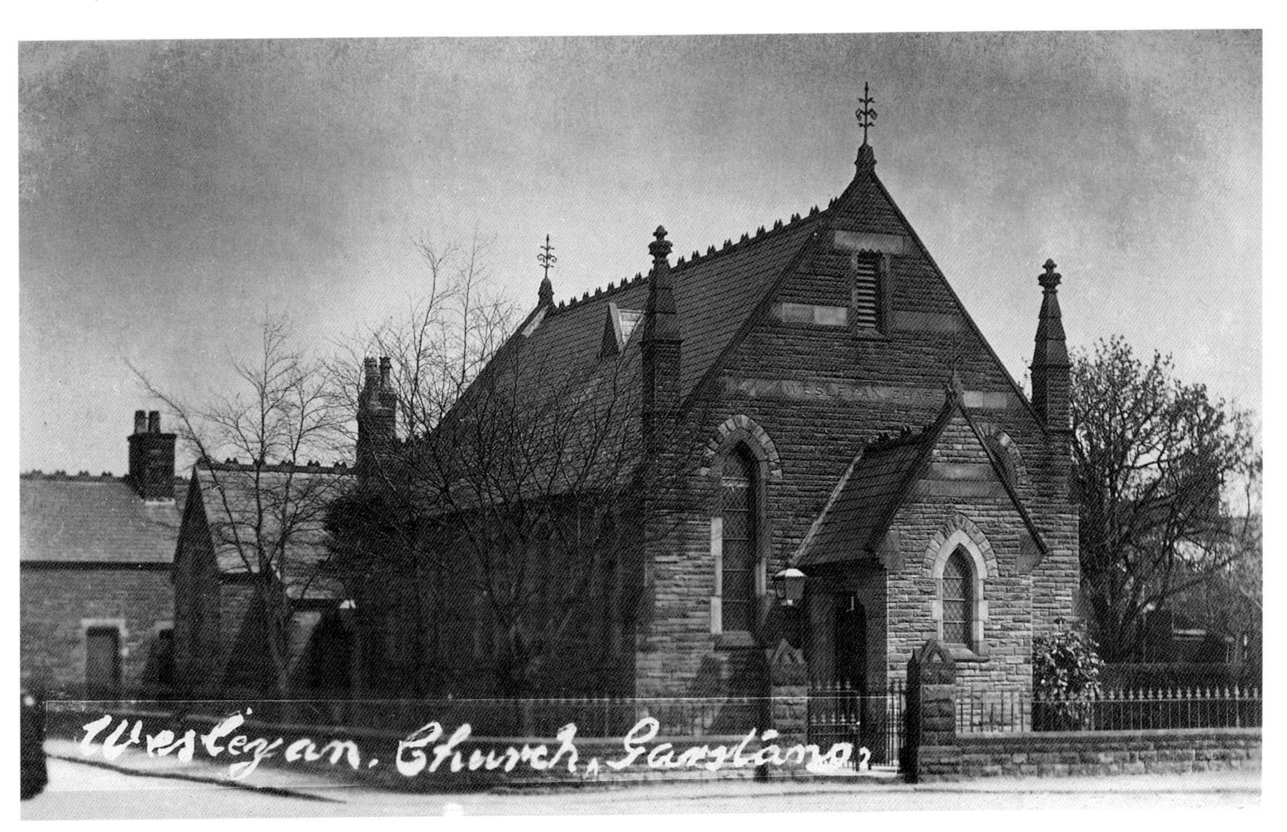

Independent (Congregational) Chapel, Garstang *(around 1910)*

The Rev. George Burder of Lancaster opened Garstang's Independent Chapel, now known as the United Reformed Church, in 1777.[145] In December 1865, at the annual Christmas tea party, a new harmonium was inaugurated in the chapel.[146] In 1867, Dr Bell, on behalf of the congregation, bought the site of the chapel from the Keppel family for £100.[147] Dr Bell practised medicine in Garstang for over 40 years. His daughter raised funds for the purchase of the site and for the renovation of the chapel, which had become dilapidated. The roof of the chapel was replaced and the interior was renovated. The restored chapel was re-opened on Monday, 13 April 1868. Around 1901, £85 was paid for a plot of land adjacent to the chapel, on which to build a new Sunday school.[148] It was also intended to use the building for tea-meetings, lectures and other social functions. After two years of raising funds towards the cost of the building, the foundation stone was laid on Wednesday, 6 May 1903. After the ceremony, tea was served in the Assembly Rooms at the Liberal Club on Bridge Street.

Garstang and Knott End Railway Bridge over the River Wyre, Garstang *(early 1900s)*

Down by the Riverside, Garstang *(photographed by H. Jackson, around 1904)*

BARNACRE AND NETHER

WYRESDALE

Castle Lane, Barnacre *(photographed by H. Jackson, around 1904)*

Castle Lane leads from the Bonds side of Wyre Bridge to Greenhalgh Castle and Castle Farm. In 1857–58, a new Catholic School and master's house were built on land in Bonds facing Castle Lane, close to the new Catholic Church.[149] In 1860, in order to improve access from Garstang to the railway, the Lancaster and Preston Railway Company offered to move the railway station closer to the town, on condition that the landowners and inhabitants of the town made a new road from Garstang to the new station.[150] The proposed site of the new station was near Turner's Bridge in Barnacre. It was proposed to build a new road from the end of Castle Lane to the new station, and to widen Castle Lane and put up a new fence.[151] Land was promised from the Barnacre Estate for the new road, and the tradesmen of Garstang raised £120 towards the cost of building it. Following negotiations, the managers of the railway company dropped the scheme due to disagreements about the proposed site of the new station.

Greenhalgh Castle, Barnacre
(photographed by F. Crosland, posted 1904)

In 1485, Thomas Stanley played a pivotal role in helping Henry Tudor to win the Battle of Bosworth Field.[152] As a reward, the new king granted him the Earldom of Derby and estates in Lancashire that had belonged to outlawed nobility. In order to protect himself from them, Thomas Stanley built Greenhalgh Castle under a licence granted by the king in 1490. During the Civil War, Greenhalgh Castle was a Royalist stronghold. Parliamentary soldiers laid siege to the castle during the winter of 1644–45. The Royalist garrison held out for several months, but eventually surrendered following the death of the governor of the castle. Around 1650, on the orders of Parliament, the castle was dismantled. Today, only the ruins of a single tower are left. Greenhalgh Castle remained the property of the Earls of Derby until around 1865, when the fourteenth Earl of Derby sold it and some adjoining land to Lord Kenlis.[153]

Castle Farm, Barnacre *(posted 1906)*

This photograph of Castle Farm was taken from just below Greenhalgh Castle, looking east towards the Bowland fells. At 11.00 p.m. on Sunday, 5 October 1862, a policeman was on duty in Barnacre when he spotted three men coming out of a field, heavily laden.[154] He searched them, and found they were carrying apples and onions, which they had stolen. The apples had been taken from the orchard of Castle Farm. One of the men escaped, while the other two were taken to the local lock-up. The following day they were sentenced to one month's imprisonment. In 1891, a fire broke out at Castle Farm.[155] Garstang Fire Brigade was brought out, and they found the roof of the property, which at that time was thatched, in flames. It took about an hour to extinguish the fire, but not before half the roof had been damaged.

Barnacre Lodge *(photographed by J. Towers, posted 1905)*

The Earl of Bective, who owned the Barnacre Estate, built Barnacre Lodge as a shooting-box between 1875 and 1878.[156] The design for the house, with its half-timbering and panels of floral decoration, was exhibited at the Royal Academy in 1877. The Earl of Bective died in 1893 at his principal residence, Underley Hall near Kirkby Lonsdale. The Countess of Bective sold the Barnacre Estate in 1899 to Thomas Rushton, a wealthy mechanical engineer from Bolton. The 1901 census shows that the family employed many servants, including a cook, five maids, a charwoman, a butler, two footmen, a coachman, three grooms, a gardener and three laundresses. For over 30 years, Mr J. Marcus Rea of Preston was agent of the Barnacre Estate.[157] When he resigned in 1905, a supper was held in his honour at the Kenlis Arms Hotel. He was presented with a mahogany clock, subscribed for by the tenants and workmen of the estate. Prizes were regularly given to tenant farmers on the Barnacre Estate, and were awarded based on the management and condition of each farm, its land and livestock.[158]

All Saints' Church, Barnacre *(photographed by H. Jackson, around 1905)*

The picturesque church of All Saints, Barnacre, was designed by Austin and Paley, a Lancaster firm of architects, and was completed in 1905. Mrs Rushton of Barnacre Lodge had the church built at a cost of about £3,000 as a memorial to her husband Thomas, who had died in 1903.[159] This photograph shows the church prior to its completion, the windows being unglazed. The church was officially opened on Friday, 28 July 1905, when the choir of St Thomas's Church, Garstang, took part in the service. The following day, Mrs Rushton entertained the tenants of the Barnacre Estate and members of the Girls' Friendly Society at Barnacre Lodge.[160] Sports were held, and tea was provided in a large marquee in the grounds. For six years, All Saints' was a chapel of ease for St Thomas's Church, Garstang. Barnacre became a separate parish in 1911 when Bishop Knox of Manchester consecrated the church.[161] Trees now obscure this view of All Saints'.

Woodacre Hall, Barnacre *(photographed by J. Towers, posted 1906)*

Woodacre Hall dates back to the thirteenth century, although the present building replaced the original hall in the seventeenth century.[162] Woodacre was once the name of a manor, and can be seen on Saxton's map of Lancashire from 1577 and Speed's map of Lancashire from 1610 as 'Waddiker'. For some time after 1712, it was home to the Duchess of Hamilton, widow of the fourth Duke of Hamilton, after he died in a duel with Lord Mohun in Hyde Park, London. In 1853, the eleventh Duke of Hamilton sold his North Lancashire property. Alderman Thompson, of Underley Hall near Kirkby Lonsdale, purchased the Barnacre portion of it, including Woodacre Hall. North of Woodacre Hall is Woodacre Great Wood, shown on Yates' map of Lancashire from 1786. It has been reduced in size by the building of the railway and motorway, but is still full of bluebells in the spring.

Crossey Gate Farm, Barnacre *(photographed by J. Towers, posted 1912)*

Crossey Gate Farm was located east of Woodacre Hall, where the public footpath alongside Long Crossey Wood meets Higher Lane, OS grid reference SD 5100 4714. Today, trees largely cover the site of the farm.

Crossey Gate, Barnacre *(photographed by J. Towers, around 1910)*

The Ford on the road to Nicky Nook, Nether Wyresdale *(photographed by H. Jackson, around 1904)*

This photograph shows an artist painting the rural view on Higher Lane, near Nicky Nook. The scene looks different today, with the stream passing under the road, and the land on the left beyond the gate covered with trees. Nicky Nook has been popular for many years with walkers and picnic parties due to the picturesque scenery, and the wonderful views over Morecambe Bay towards the Isle of Man. A botanist, visiting Nicky Nook and the Grizedale valley in 1854, recorded parts of the valley covered in wild flowers, and the air perfumed with the fragrance of wild thyme.[163] They recorded seeing plants such as ivy-leaved bellflower, cranberry and sundew in the wet areas, and carline thistle on a dry, sandy bank.

Slack Farm, Nether Wyresdale *(photographed by F. Crosland, posted 1910)*

Dating back to the seventeenth century, Slack Farm used to stand in the Grizedale valley, below Nicky Nook, OS grid reference SD 5110 4782. A public footpath runs through the site of the farm, which today is covered with grass and nettles.

Slack Farm, Nether Wyresdale *(photographed by F. Crosland, posted 1909)*

REFERENCES

1. W. Farrer (editor), *The Chartulary of Cockersand Abbey of the Premonstratensian Order: Volume I Part II* (Chetham Society, 1898), p. 280.
2. H. Fishwick, *The History of the Parish of Garstang in the County of Lancaster: Part I* (Chetham Society, 1878), pp. 5–8; A. Hewitson, *Northward* (Preston: George Toulmin, The Guardian Printing Works, 1900), p. 60; *The Preston Chronicle and Lancashire Advertiser,* 12 November 1864.
3. W. Axon, 'Chronological Notes on the Visitations of the Plague in Lancashire and Cheshire', *Transactions of the Lancashire and Cheshire Antiquarian Society*, xii (1894), pp. 54–55.
4. Fishwick, *The History of the Parish of Garstang in the County of Lancaster: Part I*, p. 8.
5. F. R. Raines (editor), *Rentale de Cokersand: being The Bursar's Rent Roll of the Abbey of Cokersand, in the County Palatine of Lancaster, for the year 1501* (Chetham Society, 1861), pp. 15–16.
6. Fishwick, *The History of the Parish of Garstang in the County of Lancaster: Part I*, pp. 15–17; Hewitson, *Northward*, p. 60; W. Farrer and J. Brownbill (editors), *The Victoria History of the County of Lancaster: Volume 7* (Archibald Constable, 1912), pp. 311–313.
7. http://www.opsi.gov.uk/chron-tables/private/p-chron12, accessed 8 March 2009.
8. Lancashire Record Office, CNP 6/1, *Confirmation of a grant by Edward II to Cockersand Abbey* (1310).
9. Fishwick, *The History of the Parish of Garstang in the County of Lancaster: Part I*, pp. 58–59.
10. Lancashire Record Office, DDX 386/8, *Garstang Corporation Records*.
11. E. Baines, *History, Directory and Gazetteer of the County Palatine of Lancaster: Volume I* (Liverpool: William Wales, 1824–25), p. 640.
12. Fishwick, *The History of the Parish of Garstang in the County of Lancaster: Part I*, p. 68.
13. *The Preston Chronicle*, 20 April 1833.
14. *The Preston Chronicle and Lancashire Advertiser*, 10 February 1872 and 6 February 1892.
15. Lancashire Record Office, DDX 386/5, *Proclamation of Garstang Fair* (1839).
16. *The Preston Chronicle and Lancashire Advertiser*, 14 July 1877.
17. *The Preston Chronicle and Lancashire Advertiser*, 14 July 1883.
18. Hewitson, *Northward*, p. 61.
19. *The Preston Chronicle and Lancashire Advertiser*, 1 December 1855 and 27 November 1869.
20. *The Preston Chronicle and Lancashire Advertiser*, 25 November 1871.
21. *The Lancaster Guardian*, 25 November 1932.
22. Lancashire Record Office, DDX 386/10, *Charity Commission Scheme for the administration of the property of the dissolved corporation* (1889).
23. http://www.visionofbritain.org.uk/text/chap_page.jsp?t_id=Fiennes&c_id=22, accessed 8 March 2009.
24. R. Patten, *The History of the Rebellion in the Year 1715* (London: James Roberts, 1745), p. 79.
25. Fishwick, *The History of the Parish of Garstang in the County of Lancaster: Part I*, p. 71.
26. *Caledonian Mercury*, 12 January 1846.
27. H. Taylor, 'The Ancient Crosses of Lancashire', *Transactions of the Lancashire and Cheshire Antiquarian Society*, xx (1902), pp. 197–199.
28. Farrer and Brownbill (editors), *The Victoria History of the County of Lancaster: Volume 7*, pp. 320–324.
29. Hewitson, *Northward*, p. 57.
30. *The Preston Chronicle and Lancashire Advertiser*, 1 July 1871.
31. Hewitson, *Northward*, pp. 68–69.
32. *The Preston Chronicle and Lancashire Advertiser*, 9 December 1876.
33. *The Preston Chronicle and Lancashire Advertiser*, 16 December 1865.
34. *The Preston Chronicle and Lancashire Advertiser*, 17 December 1870.
35. T. R. Perkins, 'The Garstang and Knot-End Railway', *Railway Magazine*, xxii (1908), pp. 72–77.
36. *The Preston Guardian*, 3 June 1911.
37. *The Lancaster Guardian*, 17 June 1911.
38. *The Lancaster Guardian*, 24 June 1911.
39. *The Lancaster Guardian*, 8 July 1911.
40. Hewitson, *Northward*, p. 48.
41. *The Preston Chronicle and Lancashire Advertiser*, 13 September 1873.
42. Hewitson, *Northward*, p. 50.
43. *The Preston Chronicle and Lancashire Advertiser*, 7 March 1857.
44. *The Preston Guardian*, 4 March 1905.
45. *The St. James's Chronicle or, British Evening-Post*, 16–18 April 1793.
46. *The Preston Chronicle and Lancashire Advertiser*, 17 May 1856.
47. *The Preston Chronicle and Lancashire Advertiser*, 31 December 1892.
48. *The Statutes of the United Kingdom of Great Britain and Ireland, 12 & 13 Victoria* (Her Majesty's Printers, 1849), pp. 377–378.
49. Hewitson, *Northward*, p. 3.
50. *The Lancaster Guardian*, 27 October 1928.
51. Lancashire Record Office, DDX 194/22, *Strip plan of roads: Ellel Moor to Howath Moor, Howath Moor to Preston* (1684).
52. *The Lancaster Guardian*, 18 November 1905.
53. *The Preston Chronicle and Lancashire Advertiser*, 21 August 1858.
54. *The Preston Chronicle and Lancashire Advertiser*, 21 October 1865.
55. *The Preston Guardian*, 9 June 1906.
56. *The Liverpool Mercury*, 14 March 1834 and 15 August 1834; *The Morning Chronicle*, 14 March 1834 and 16 August 1834.
57. *The Preston Chronicle and Lancashire Advertiser*, 7 February 1846.
58. *The Preston Chronicle and Lancashire Advertiser*, 30 April 1859.
59. *The Preston Chronicle and Lancashire Advertiser*, 4 August 1866.
60. *The Preston Chronicle and Lancashire Advertiser*, 22 April 1893.
61. Hewitson, *Northward*, p. 59.
62. *The Lancaster Guardian*, 16 October 1897.
63. *Kelly's Directory of Lancashire* (1905), p. 498.
64. *Cook's Lancaster and District Directory* (1896), p.256.
65. *The Preston Guardian*, 1 June 1901.
66. *The Preston Guardian*, 25 May 1907.
67. *The Prrston Chronicle and Lancashire Advertiser*, 16 February 1861.
68. Hewitson, *Northward*, p. 64.
69. *The Preston Chronicle and Lancashire Advertiser*, 20 July 1867.
70. A. Hewitson, *Our Country Churches and Chapels* (Preston: Chronicle Office, 1872), p. 477.
71. *The Preston Chronicle and Lancashire Advertiser*, 24 June 1893.
72. Hewitson, *Our Country Churches and Chapels*, p. 477.

73. *The Preston Chronicle and Lancashire Advertiser*, 6 November 1841.
74. Hewitson, *Our Country Churches and Chapels*, p. 480
75. *The Preston Chronicle and Lancashire Advertiser*, 23 January 1847.
76. *The Preston Chronicle and Lancashire Advertiser*, 30 December 1848; W. B. Porteus, *Notes on the History of St. Thomas' Church, Garstang* (1970), p. 12.
77. *The Preston Chronicle and Lancashire Advertiser*, 6 March 1875.
78. Porteus, *Notes on the History of St. Thomas' Church, Garstang*, p. 13.
79. Porteus, *Notes on the History of St. Thomas' Church, Garstang*, p. 16.
80. Lancashire Record Office, DDX 131/1, *Particulars and Plan of the Garstang Manor Estate to be sold by auction* (1919).
81. *The Preston Chronicle and Lancashire Advertiser*, 15 December 1877.
82. Porteus, *Notes on the History of St. Thomas' Church, Garstang*, p. 15.
83. *The Preston Chronicle and Lancashire Advertiser*, 30 December 1865.
84. Porteus, *Notes on the History of St. Thomas' Church, Garstang*, p. 15.
85. *The Preston Guardian*, 11 March 1905.
86. *The Preston Chronicle and Lancashire Advertiser*, 13 September 1873.
87. Hewitson, *Our Country Churches and Chapels*, p. 467.
88. *The Preston Chronicle and Lancashire Advertiser*, 15 November 1879; *The Liverpool Mercury*, 1 December 1879.
89. *The Preston Chronicle and Lancashire Advertiser*, 19 September 1891.
90. *Cook's Lancaster and District Directory* (1896), p.256.
91. Hewitson, *Northward*, p. 61.
92. Baines, *History, Directory and Gazetteer of the County Palatine of Lancaster: Volume I*, p. 640.
93. *The Preston Chronicle*, 10 September 1831.
94. *History, Topography and Directory of Westmorland with Lonsdale and Amounderness in Lancashire* (Mannex & Co., 1851), p. 560.
95. Lancashire Record Office, DDX 386/8, *Garstang Corporation Records*.
96. Hewitson, *Northward*, p. 61.
97. *The Lancaster Guardian*, 7 August 1897.
98. *The Lancaster Guardian*, 26 June 1897.
99. Hewitson, *Northward*, p. 61.
100. *The Lancaster Guardian*, 2 September 1905.
101. *The Preston Chronicle and Lancashire Advertiser*, 10 March 1855.
102. *The Preston Chronicle and Lancashire Advertiser*, 16 July 1859.
103. *The Lancaster Guardian*, 26 May 1906.
104. *The True Briton*, 9 April 1799.
105. *The Preston Chronicle*, 12 January 1839.
106. *The Preston Chronicle and Lancashire Advertiser*, 30 April 1859.
107. *The Preston Guardian*, 2 July 1927.
108. *The Northern Star and Leeds General Advertiser*, 3 December 1842.
109. *The Preston Chronicle and Lancashire Advertiser*, 27 November 1861.
110. *The Preston Chronicle and Lancashire Advertiser*, 17 February 1872.
111. *The Preston Chronicle and Lancashire Advertiser*, 4 April 1874.
112. *The Preston Chronicle and Lancashire Advertiser*, 23 December 1876.
113. *The Preston Chronicle and Lancashire Advertiser*, 24 December 1881.
114. *The Preston Chronicle and Lancashire Advertiser*, 29 December 1877.
115. Lancashire Record Office, DDX 386/8, *Garstang Corporation Records*.
116. *The Preston Chronicle and Lancashire Advertiser*, 5 May 1877.
117. *The Preston Chronicle and Lancashire Advertiser*, 3 May 1879.
118. Hewitson, *Northward*, p. 63.
119. *The Preston Chronicle*, 5 July 1834.
120. *The Preston Chronicle and Lancashire Advertiser*, 10 September 1870.
121. Hewitson, *Northward*, p. 60.
122. Lancashire Record Office, DDX 1096/12, *Sale Catalogue of the Lordship of Garstang* (1867).
123. *The Preston Chronicle and Lancashire Advertiser*, 18 February 1865.
124. *The Preston Chronicle and Lancashire Advertiser*, 25 February 1865.
125. Lancashire Record Office, DDX 131/1, *Particulars and Plan of the Garstang Manor Estate to be sold by auction* (1919).
126. *The Preston Chronicle and Lancashire Advertiser*, 29 November 1845.
127. Lancashire Record Office, DDX 386/8, *Garstang Corporation Records*.
128. H. Taylor, 'The Ancient Crosses of Lancashire', *Transactions of the Lancashire and Cheshire Antiquarian Society*, xx (1902), pp. 197–199.
129. *The Preston Chronicle and Lancashire Advertiser*, 12 November 1870, 9 November 1872, 8 November 1873, 7 November 1874, 9 November 1878 and 12 November 1881.
130. Hewitson, *Our Country Churches and Chapels*, p. 492.
131. *The Preston Chronicle and Lancashire Advertiser*, 27 November 1875.
132. *The Preston Chronicle and Lancashire Advertiser*, 10 February 1872.
133. *The Preston Chronicle and Lancashire Advertiser*, 23 June 1883.
134. *The Lancaster Guardian*, 9 June 1906.
135. Lancashire Record Office, DDX 386/1, *Sir Edward Walpole to the Bailiff and Burgesses of Garstang: Lease for 200 years of a piece of waste ground called Croston's Waste on which to erect a school* (1756).
136. Hewitson, *Northward*, p. 61.
137. Hewitson, *Our Country Churches and Chapels*, p. 471.
138. *The Preston Chronicle and Lancashire Advertiser*, 27 December 1873.
139. *The Preston Chronicle and Lancashire Advertiser*, 29 March 1879.
140. *The Preston Chronicle and Lancashire Advertiser*, 3 December 1892.
141. *The Lancaster Gazette*, 19 November 1831.
142. *The Preston Chronicle and Lancashire Advertiser*, 27 April 1878.
143. *The Lancaster Guardian*, 27 April 1878.
144. *The Preston Chronicle and Lancashire Advertiser*, 21 December 1878.
145. Hewitson, *Our Country Churches and Chapels*, p. 482.
146. *The Preston Chronicle and Lancashire Advertiser*, 30 December 1865.
147. *The Preston Chronicle and Lancashire Advertiser*, 18 April 1868.
148. *The Lancaster Guardian*, 9 May 1903.
149. *The Preston Chronicle and Lancashire Advertiser*, 21 August 1858.
150. *The Preston Chronicle and Lancashire Advertiser*, 20 October 1860, 17 November 1860 and 22 November 1862.
151. *The Preston Chronicle and Lancashire Advertiser*, 29 November 1862.
152. Hewitson, *Northward*, pp. 53–55.
153. *The Preston Chronicle and Lancashire Advertiser*, 16 December 1865.
154. *The Preston Chronicle and Lancashire Advertiser*, 11 October 1862.
155. *The Preston Chronicle and Lancashire Advertiser*, 4 April 1891.
156. Hewitson, *Northward*, pp. 68–69.
157. *The Preston Guardian*, 4 March 1905.
158. *The Preston Guardian*, 22 April 1905.
159. *The Lancaster Guardian*, 5 August 1905.
160. *The Lancaster Standard and County Advertiser*, 4 August 1905.
161. Porteus, *Notes on the History of St. Thomas' Church, Garstang*, p. 14.
162. Farrer and Brownbill (editors), *The Victoria History of the County of Lancaster: Volume 7*, pp. 315–320; Hewitson, *Northward*, pp. 66–67.
163. *The Preston Chronicle and Lancashire Advertiser*, 23 September 1854.